T0162101

WESTE

RNPRA

CTICE

WESTERN

PRACTICE

Stephen Motika

Alice James Books
FARMINGTON, MAINE

10 9 8 7 6 5 4 3 2 1

Alice James Books are published by Alice James Poetry Cooperative, Inc.,
an affiliate of the University of Maine at Farmington.

ALICE JAMES BOOKS
238 MAIN STREET
FARMINGTON, ME 04938
www.alicejamesbooks.org

Library of Congress Cataloging-in-Publication Data
Motika, Stephen, 1977-
 Western practice / by Stephen Motika.
    p. cm.
 ISBN 978-1-882295-91-3 (pbk.)
 I. Title.
 PS3613.O835W47 2012
 811'.6--dc23
                                2011049180

Alice James Books gratefully acknowledges support from individual donors, private foundations,
the University of Maine at Farmington and the National Endowment for the Arts. ❦

Image of Alice James by permission of the Houghton Library, Harvard University.
Call number: pf MS Am 1094, Box 3 (44d)

Cover Art: *Mount Tamalpais* by Eadweard Muybridge (1830-1904)

CONTENTS

ACKNOWLEDGMENTS

An earlier version of "Ocean Park" appeared in *Other Times*, published at the University of Nevada, Las Vegas, in 2008. Thanks to editor Simon Horning.

Earlier versions of "walk & ferry" and "sun in" were published in *Eleven Eleven*. Thanks to poetry editor Thomas Rees.

"Pacific Slope" was published in *The Brooklyn Review*. Thanks to poetry editor Ted Dodson.

"Delusion's Enclosure: on Harry Partch (1901 - 1974)" was published in October 2011 in *At Length*. Thanks to editor Jonathan Farmer.

Thanks are due to my family, friends, teachers, and colleagues for encouraging this work. I'm especially grateful to the faculty at Brooklyn College, my authors and fellow editors at Nightboat Books, and the staff and patrons of Poets House. Thanks to the board and staff of Alice James Books and to the Lower Manhattan Cultural Council for providing me with a 2010-2011 *Workspace* Residency, where I completed this book. I'm indebted to Jill Magi and Abraham Avnisan Nowitz for their close readings and to all the Californians in my life, especially my parents. This book is for them, and for Photi, who shares with me the daily practice of living.

For my parents

and for Photi

I

You can tell by the eucalyptus tree, its shaggy branches scatter buttons. In the afternoons, when the shades were pulled for my nap, the light coming through was of a dark yellow, nearly orange, melancholy, as heavy as honey, and it made me thirsty. That doesn't say it all, or even a greater part.

—LYN HEJINIAN

early hour, resistant to time, an arrival. people out of rooms and gathered, four now, to eat. with florist at table, a dining out & bowl of dahlias.

expect to be nervous in the beginning.

underground, underwater.

I meant to burrow under it and sleep.

crepes for dinner and drinks with thirsty boy, intern and radical, poet and usurper, intake, of knowing much more than I do, all these relevant things.

he returned to his friend & together they started to race up the hill.

later, we lay sleepless, knowing, to pick up and put the desire and excitement down, that a book about Florentine history might be the only thing, to rest it all for a bit.

to account for the origin of that marvel resulted in myths.

gray awareness, bay, city, and bridge, reaching like twine. feed the fowl, the tortoise, a slipping away to hiding cat.

to be living with nature.

the rest of rest, riding back, the heavy lidded quiet, in the rush of tunnel, of movement, of distinct locations passing as platforms.

the scene was in the center of the road; I left it & sat on the curb.

the currying of fruit picked from trees, passion fruit vines spilling through the window.

the words of our mouths.

to lie by heavy apples, horses grazing and pears in mouth. artichoke, rosemary in rows, quiet fields with the final fading. earth, green of summer, dust dry, bone dry, yellowed grass, pipe quiet.

the farm possibly unusual.

treasure of exhaustion; recounted the sadness of the fathers and of the men, of being lost in the ether there.

if you dream you're dressed, you see a picture.

rain came, a heavy blinding rain. water rushed off roofs, splattered down gutters and into streets. wet feet and pants.

I who come from the clear font.

shoals   in sparked night
real creatures crushed by

                heated hunter
                   gathers me, in long stocking

pearlescent, feasting
                  salty heat of
abalone
      stewed in derelict measure

climbed, naked, on board
             each body, a mosaic in sand

drift, sea rind, carapace in hand
              to which we, a fire

red carved, each tissue ripped from small purse
                  tessellated surface
     talus shade

        in tears

(i)

remembered those
    lakes
                reedy washing basins
    sandy
    stepped
        aside those red rusted
            museums
            nineteenth century pavilions
        corroded promenades

    in our time
        in small suit
            likes of chess   men
                and eyes
    in irrevocable position(s)
                yellow tripped
      to underpass

in duck beneath
    skin sifting between   fingertips
      pulled hush of train
        passing
    a metallic regularity
        body in motion
    miming

(ii)

how did the little one give way to chest hair and strides

                  mustachioed San Franciscan
                  drugged a brilliant

                      dancing man in yoga suit
so many
          color wheels
a face

what excitement in pain :

                      walk through
                            a cosmos

                unutterable this lover
                    aside from red seats in 16mm shadow
          footsteps up Nob hill
                the town where we made up
    sun sinks quickly
        cap of smog
                  so lovely
                  so sick

        that part inside BART where coffee made you inside out
          and aside were stacks of days of years
             numbers for those that made
sense
             some attempt to reach
                  out of reach
distant limb
        sea breeze too can make
     us   quieter
              in blurred prints

(iii)

type

     moving   along

                  quadrants

        (finding)

laced libraries made against

        Division's long reach to worry

           visit staircases

              boy's packed bags

        angry old professor

           indeed Lorca's

              fear of women

              forsake fears for men

arcs   after summer rain   a doppelgänger these rainbows

        letters never rested so well

           we'll make

              divers for the lake

              thirsty for

              lovely athleticism

              & incubation

                            skin

        inspections lined up

        vertical features

              achieved off the

                page

        wrists

        bound   bonded

held back

        again held breath

           our waiting

           our insistence taking

we
in amber

sandy wood speaks   tongue

road
ways
through   news
papers

how the ache of beauty makes you sick

glasses sparkle   fire
side

dry lick of facing
animals
down a
circumference

luminescent

ran along

lake
shore

not yet   icy

I took this via Bixby
cross
madrone-
faced   TAIN

IN wet tongue rainy

por/poise
ride a kelp/bed away

WE path insistent
sun

garnet   ENTHUSED

missive REMEMBER spree

breath * recapit-

WAY   marks us time

if by road scenery   by

walking "beach comb"

spring snakes

HOLD   (us)
away

I lay   immersed

                    moonfaced
                       shirtless
                          in amaryllis

PINK   naked not ladies

exhausts us   ELEVATED

        ribbons twist   "lance"

                              mineral bath

yellow   channel

        this

        speaking

heavily (heavenly)   rest a wrest

tree branches combed into coves   in tender green

                enriched columns

                fall through stable floor

seize limbs

        hair

    track   what a muddy boot

a foot print in the lair of ardor   debauch

    still the tin of (this) kitchen

    still consider colored tape and

        infrastructure

vessel travel   rocking

    a bit boaty

        roars with lasso and zoom exhaust

    relief   a stolen fuel filled transformer

    red   take a car out of the garage

the language of "ego" without tea or medication

    fancy these brown trousers

        petals

dealt to delta
sky of buildings

      small bodies held in smaller beds
            recognizable idioms

      lines of little books
                    gasoline residuals from road-
                         way
ficus trees
      torn ligaments of childhood

walls
  creepers
      reject

      this task reminds us
               marbled columbarium
                fern plantings
               Olmstead fountains

                          an instinct
                           red-haired
                           lineages

                bay
                  interior nests

                  towns
                    where our mothers came from

                    orchards
                     & palms

TEA PALINODE (18ᵀᴴ & SANCHEZ)

In removing sidewalks from San Francisco, I planted trees, oaks and laurel.
An arc by bay, I sat in parallel time, scratching the Velcro clasp of revealing
and not revealing. Having made amends in a small space, we stepped lakeside,
fostered beads and tears. The mist of God fell away, the paralysis instilled;
I walked alone, books on fern morphology in hand, until the region of lawns
unrolled. Tending to death, this untouched shade, we troubled, uncoupled.
Lost to sweep of Queen Anne's lace and leaflets, our errant grip slips, slack.
Wrapped in English, sleep exhumed a theory at map's edge, cast in ornament,
artifice, my tongue an observer.

"This is my trinity: sound-magic, visual beauty, experience-ritual."
–Harry Partch

I.

a gist (of origin) to say born Oaklandia on 6.24.01

      later

            child of deserts

                "the dying gasps of the old West"

         'til in Tucson

              Benson (three hundred people and eleven saloons)

      & @ Albuquerque

    in nights, long freight trains passing
              antiphonal then

                  steam whistle 60 miles yonder

small garden : Phoenix : rising, then falling

                books in Mandarin

           (parents who lost their missionary zeal)

trips to Kansas City & musical studies & jobs as porters

      but at 14, he knew that it was   SOUND

II.

what early music?

    hymns
    Chinese lullabies
    Yaqui Indian puberty rituals
    Hebrew chants
    Edison cylinder records
    Okie songs
            (working the vineyards)

took a trashing from proper musical lessons in Los Angeles but

                        no
                        deep
                        &
                        abiding
                        tie

mother struck dead by a streetcar

father dead a couple of yrs

age 20 / alone from there on and ever

this young metropolis and trips to Philharmonic hall

                triumphant   love
                    a roll/hay roll with
                        lost
                    Ramón Novarro
    (murdered by two hustlers four decades later)

            always a love for the body

III.

with parts

       p-a-r-t-c-h

          study : history of tone

        fifty-three tone system proposed   by the Chinese in the first century
                                        by Nicolas Mercator in the 17th

- microtonal mishaps in the west -

     as if to say

                   just-intonational scales

then to New Orleans and New York and London and Malta

      a return to

    Li Po verse
        on adapted viola

    where do you live?
               off a city street
         and ten thousand houses among drooping willows

1930-1947 singing Biblical passages, hitch-hiker transcripts.

                   Why all the trouble?

   MUSIC

     "a language in itself"

IV.

Greek &
Noh
drama,

Japanese
kabuki

Mummer's
plays

CREATION

dramas containing music, dance, mime, shouting, whistling, and slapstick

so early (to have known) so late (to have been discovered to have known)

V.

back from San Joaquin

(keeping music in hobo bundle)

at Big Sur
    coast work camp
        met Jean Varda

an understanding, as if to say we're in   synchrony
                            synchromy
                                  for painters

always loving, loving, loving, loving
                        (men)

VI. BITTER MUSIC (DEPRESSION ERA SUITE)

- alpha -

convict camps, coast of magnificent
                              descend-
                              ings

                                        CALI
                                          down

black mountain to coast(line)

                                   every starry
                                          whiten
                                          ed

                                          ridge

            clasp
            coast road
                              in moves north
                                          and east
return south to

- beta -

warm (to) sleeping bag

                 Pablo's soup in hand

                          willowed sands

                                 river side

    entihillion stars

                    "Why wander?"

       gone away for-ever

                          in the eternity of infinity

          & thumb my nose at tomorrow

- gamma -

Slate's hot springs

           long since
                    dead

an ownership   a Bright Angel leads to the baths

                          on board to Big Creek (wink, wink)

evening campfire, San Simon

                  at Cone Peak

- delta -

at Ojai dry leaved pepper tree body

                    riddled white snaked water
             in the blackness
      an inky o-high oak
         a beauty of hands stroke

VII.

        August beach, ocean breath

Mount Diablo
        sinking beneath the horizon

                            stay & move

              to pass peak

                 with men

            food and flops and "well-made chaps"

                                   yes yes
                                       all this
                               brazen talk

        by creeks and woodsheds and more along side the highway

VIII.

to make:

                    "U.S. Highball," hobo trip with music

        going East mister? (plucked)

                Freeze another night tonight

        Stay out of Denver

                It moves back and forth

        Is that blanket big enough for two?

                Chicago, Chicago, Chicago

end at Sparks division yards

IX.

in   red-
            wood

            groves of

            euca-
            lypt

                    after several durations at Ithaca and Madison

                         for isolation, interview

                              founded his instrument workshop

"a philosophical man seduced into carpentry"

                    river camper
                    woodworker

"an acoustical ardor and a conceptual fervor"

            tuning: total gambit of dissonance and consonance

X.

Orchestra at Gualala:

    a. zymo-xyl

        "exercise in hither and thither aesthesia"
        with kettle top, oak block, on hubcap, wine and booze bottles

    b. Gourd Tree Gong

        twelve bells (exotic fruit) on eucalypt bar
            & piece of aircraft bomber

    c. Mazda Marimba

        god of light sounds like the percolations of a coffee pot

    d. Spoils of Wars

        seven brass artillery casings hanging "instead of
        shredding young men's bodies on the battle field"

    e. Cloud-Chamber Bowls

        chemical-solution jars from the university's radiation lab

XI.

activation of investigation and interventions with Yeats

and enticement

HP: "I have read his prefaces—I love his prefaces, incidentally."

WBY: "A California musician called a few days ago and is coming again tomorrow. He is working on the relation between words and music…. He speaks to this instrument."

HP: "The minute I brought out my viola and sang, Yeats just loved it. He's not one for theory."

the taking of Oedipus an opera written.

happily written here, the land of no there there.

XII.

compelled by kithara

Partch built a great lyre of 72 strings.

Orpheus's lyre had three stings.

Timotheus (446-357 BC), who dared to expand the scale on the Kithara by adding four strings to the eight approved by Pythagoras was driven out of Sparta forever.

"These days, when someone does something different, they ignore him to death."

XIII.

intoned dialogue god, then help us assemble

by way of chorus

Oh— Oh— Oh— Ah— Ah— Ah—

in way of supplicant's branches

with such cries of sorrow

good news of lights, curtains

suffering in homeless sea, thunder, lightning, lost to

as "death himself is dead"

Tiresias, presented by spokesman,
regales Creon

anger of mattering, basest of men,

a filling
this rage
against

evidence of
proof?

a tumult of iron, prophets forgotten

Oh- Oh   Lo-   Oh-   Lo- Oh-where is Bold Oedipus?

(quick sketches by Lebrun, Baskin, Kolwitz)

appointed end, free from   pain

XIV.

euphoric

    aside
    warehouse
        descending
        narrow
        stairway

            in scene six from 1956

    baroque leaps

"Anyone can dream of bringing control to a Sausalito love affair."

           but only the witch can accomplish it.

XV.

       back from Urbana:

Ancient Chorus in "Revelation in the Courthouse Park"

                this palace
                alights to be seen by

                          piccolo
                transient

                (Dionysus, Pentheus, Agave, Cadmus,
                Tiresias, Guard, Herdsmen, and Chorus)

                Greek melodrama arrived in
                rural Illinois

                kithara & instruments

here, on the seventh day,

        petals

        fell on

        Petaluma

                in voiceless score

XVI.

west Los Angeles boulevard:

chromelodeon, counts six 2/1 harmonium

collapsed
                    a monophony: the might of the HUMAN e-a-r

the breeze as perceived by Marin Mersenne, on the throat.

                    equivocation of the *klang*

                              in components of tone

in ratios,
                    cycles
in intervals,
                    immediacy
in frequencies
                    systems
in procedures,
                    limits

                    tasks to Pasadena Museum

All to be tasked by "Delusions' Fury," chance dramas on stage.

HP: *I would choose to be anonymous.*
        Who cares who wrote it?
        Who cares what the name was?

XVII.

The Dreamer that Remains

Viet's time

soul's chance, five decades apart, was Stephen Pouliot

"turn left on Orpheus Drive, left on Sunset"
in this small town

Pacific, a sexy beach

where, to find

Peace
Love

stairway's chant

volcanic Harry: looking down, laughing

Etruscan touchstone

XVIII.

how to see him, on film, all too late

        kimono purple
             Partch sees
                      a loss of rose petal jam
      a harmonic convergence

in this study for loving (underwritten by Betty Freeman):

        in red/yellow/pale blue tank tops & jeans

            a set of constructions to hold beautiful boys
              in floating atmosphere of white
                   at San Diego State

"tongue must couple with the cavity or there's no resonant tone. yes, this is sexy."

XIX.

and with Lou Harrison

       stackside, found each other in the SF public library

              clearing house for books, for s-x years

    to speak to each other.
             mentorship. of generosity. and. of knowing.

      teased about inflexibility of his "systems"

        hosted in redwood park

XX.

1974: back again: *Genesis of Music* springs from the *Dreamers* creation.

"Note: the widely current practice of using the word note to indicate a musical sound, or pitch, is not followed in this work."

final interview after interview, lost road, the sign ever propped before

generation of youth

LISTEN TO THAT

pied piper

red-lamped night

shaded Socrates

looking out, a letter to the world, in this enclosure.

"I went outside. I'm still going outside."

II

I feel I'm in a slingshot – a loop

is.

there's
no relation to one's eyes –

just go out.

—LESLIE SCALAPINO

I.

            in Ocean Park
            and because of dim sum

            green leg with
                        white
                              stripes

a stipulation
            so that shoes and
                        green shirts
                        tresseled

shredding but not carrots
                        in a concave
                              sense

remember foot-
            steps & palms

                                    fallen fronds
                                    fallen house   .

            sailboats sharp, triangle as pattered

                  sand dimpled
                        by water by waves

what horse and what sound
what: speaker and jester
eyebrow and light

            steps
            sits

yellow roof
yellow

        seasoned
        creature with hum in motor

            in fistful, green bolted, ochre

     redder, reddening
                in apogee
                    treating the edged like a friend

II.

                                        where to be into there
how

hearing skateboards

                                        sun fall finally
                                        air crisps

                              sitting concrete warm schoolyard gravel
                              footsteps crested little hill

with cut roadway

                              looming park

shaded spaces   you
        wait

remembering the sea unseeable

                                        for shining
                                        grime
                                        salt
                                        vapor
                                        for diesel droning

must call

III.

brought noir   in Chandler pages

yellow cover   coveted

                            a poor read
                                somehow

read   &   watched

furtively (up) and (down)   within eyes

Marlowe's footsteps   errant visit
                            blocks away

to Zuckies
    orange letters

a carved agave   photoing leafy sword
                            punctured hearts

eucalyptal shade   mothy
                     grassy

thousands   fruit fallen
                lawn stretched

                          inedible & bright

drying thread structures

        how do you talk   to the man   with bags
                           of magazines
                             years
                               of traveling
                      heavy glasses

cerulean
      a caesura

     silent
     too   as two more than

              these
              towers
  ala Simon Rodia

houseboat walker

     inclined creator of   survive

            suspended   a cylindrical
                   a spiral

    on horizon
Gabes chapped   white
            suspension
              in terrier
   ineffable
      cars go

          off tufts
              en
              broken
                  against gain
cement stained
      a violent cuff

     rust face within fence

   running high above
          high-
          desert places

1955

Hopps' Syndell Studio, discreet 'nuff stuff… as to say make it man. count the actions

      1. at the merry go round. a fine building.
          met Kerouac, Ginsberg, no shit
          even Cassady

      2. round and round

did you always drive then? with Kaufman, post nuclear Futurist… saw the DeFeo, *Untitled-Tree*, lost in columnar woods

          lie down
          oleander
          crushed in pinks   whites

      scratch this away

      graffiti and pulpy leaves : nopales too

                      gape

                      face down

all these missing boys, girls… too much for me. but *Semina*—a sudden illumination of ones and twos. ranks envelopes with string. Berman, Herms at the Baza Shack. old oils drenched. carbonated. picked up Dean for a ride. ambiance of walking man, little ceramic Voulkos with ties, Price before the price was paid.

1956

Jazz days, we saw Mingus, day before last in tan trench, coasts and cats, Art Pepper walking hills, hilling in, tel-, phone polls, long boots, to take… mystery… all low rides. fuller life, all this, full, instant, theater, a "now" gallery working, knowing now.

Fuller. Ferus. find. fisting fast. feasting fat. fats. on the road alongside cat in the hat.

police actions. in red nightmare of shut down, shut off, take an escape these, in veritas, panel, lost, temple, apprehension (& allegory), ill-timed to set rigors down laurel, the canyon, in wreath, lonely—sleeping—over. for.

1957

Mr. Coleman's Something Else, at Venice, all West, East-West west, greasy tracks, xpress
tracks, express-o, press a coffee. X. holy barbarians vs. the smog inspector. many vs. one.
sent him away. more at Gas House blue, prefigure more than Light and Space. Palms, grass,
every crazy face. sand house with sea cast. ice plants. sunny alley aside Perkoff's tricks, flicks.
trickster harsh in heroin haze "love, of the place, the real place"

    take on "what a city
            is"

1958

driving/free-
               some/for/of
                       -dom
                                   stars/rats

man/a   thunder

                       this bird with clean-edged forms, modern, always MAN, take
this

        COLOR-FORM

                     matters not the connection

                                 show (abstract) up shape

1959

chemical shade

        spheres

               violet
               chartreuse
               neon, internal engine
                        space driven,
                                   cyclonic ride

                    Chemosphere A-N-D Jupiter C

Mr. Schulman took us there. hat and sunglass. rode a wheelie for

                     a little missing man,

            suburban, righteous, but somehow above

                        (San Fernando)

1.) the Koenig: housewives, rubber plants, disintegrated fracture of modernist kit

2.) architecture for war machines, double, hay curtain, they'll take this to
                                  Viet-
                                  nam

1960

free
way(s)

fly
way(s)

swept in full (flood), racing arcs of left/right

ever   eye

distance in, ahead

A.) gradient
B.) ramp
C.) merge

like Larry Bell's Orphan Annie. high kite orange. such edge, Bengston's red
orange

The Eds crash the sack, rash tack, a big mack

soak in Adorno trash, kulture vulture, right here in Slow Cal

mystic | gather

1961

Yves Klein blue /radiance of number /all chemical / alchemical

    ventriloquial venture

        Eames through and through

in Venice

        disaster strike like snakes

fire 1	flood 1
fire 2	flood 2

surf these licking flames? waves? mad men on boards one too many times.

early Irwin and McLaughlin's ever yellow black white yellow yellows

        tell us the culture

1962

Tinguely de Saint Phalle (Niki Niki) with rifles. LA style, aside

                              HEAVY INDUSTRY   the
goodlookin Oklahoman walked in the room.

                                        So much to say in STANDARD (English)
                                        petroleum man's good fortune. shut up: it's all
                                        a DOUBLE STANDARD

take the milk bottle, blue and rippled, the magazine, certain forums, too much   SPAM

              brushed away the studios perfect haze, the description of collections

        Kienholz, Idaho man, dancing the whisky, night bourbon dance.

                                        crawl inside & lie down against the future

1963

dam burst in City of Night.

Duchamp in gracious-ladied Pasadena

    Backus (Bacchus), another gardener, spoke every day to Marcel, in walking shoes.
    From hotel greens, the gardens of Hotel Green.
    Greener than verifax and fax: collage of the faceless.

Foulkes, boy artist in Chavez Ravine

    painting postcard. an American original. really. rusted. sepia.

   "We can only applaud."   (masonite finish)

       and for what?

1964

Gehry @ Danziger house
                encanyoned, alcoving

Martins @ Water & Power
                in pleated fountains

Ruscha @ LACMA
                and burning bldgs

"seems like a good way to start"

        Barney's Beanery *always fun*

        the first picture, plastic trees, smokes and eats and drinks.
        EK here, all here, Hollywood Hills here, always, dried laminates, here.

swimming in water pool. Hockney pools. aside, boys inside, for enriched viewing.

Celmins: gun with hand. white visions. violent visions. a Billy club in face vision.

1965

dissent and vision, you know, like, S=T=O=P this W=A=R

WATTS WAR

May 7 : Insurrection

the six long August days of Burn, Baby, Burn

"no way to delay trouble coming everyday"

take this tv note, Echo Park notes, but still leaves 34 dead, Zappa or no Zappa

Noah Purifoy's pinecone for children. Artist in off hours, but

& Corita (Sister Mary)

who came out of the water

1966

artists   an anti-war infrastructure of pro TEST

(like large George Rickey – polls + beams = types of towers)

ok, a soft telegram of *solidarité*

in the Free Press we learn of the press' downplay, playing down

a missed exercise
The Wild Angels
location, location, locations

Pynchon's "Watts is tough" resists the unreal. riot as art (chaos)

realize this: remember the music.

or 66 signs of Neon.

1967

Nin in The Garden of Eden
                    an effect(ive) gesture   so many more pools
                                                                      so little rain

in ochre swirls, a lacework
                    of water
                                        en (bodied) aqua. tanner's wah-wah.

                                                    all the while, a

Huxley's ride, deserts, in hill house hideaway.

                                        in lovely death

                              far above parking lots

                                                    aerial

                              "throw a typewriter out the window"

then FLUIDS: Kaprow's melting

                                        shirtless with bricks

                                                    face I—furrow furred I—faux

                                        smoggy palmed stage to make ice
                                                    palace
                                                              happening

1968

with brown berets... EAST LA blowouts.

(an over time) situation

La Causa & clinic

chicanito &
involv-ations

march for the soul (soledad) of la

to have been – utopian if

of AN action (s)

what about Baldessari's WRONG

or a viewpoint on "what to leave out: the eye"

1969

a bldg. of new art schools. a disney school… for the arts. california arts.

then Ruppersberg on location:

"my shows could be carried around in a briefcase."

and David Hammons' black hands on white door. admissions door.

Turrell arrives at Mendota hotel for light stoppage, sky drawing

Ocean Park, California

operative blues: *Reamar Blue / Rondo Double, Pale Blue*

Maria Nordman's Moveable Walls
(& very different from)

1970

tendency for
                pink sky and orange sun on
                                "and why not"

does the LA air lie in its lair? this tricky valentine, icebag on the way to our day hikes

        "They're like painting, like visions." -Celmins (in translation)

or Bas boy Jan Ader NOT making body art with views and visions

or David Hammons body prints: Slauson (Ave.) studio. beard brushing /paper touching;
margarine impression. pigment blooms sprinkling.

                                but in *Real Life*, "I can't stand art."

1971

Judy's in the ring, Cal State ring. No punching. No Cohen either.

        You've been to Chicago?
        Yeah, you?
        Nah, just born there.
        Yeah.

now Reyner Banham's here; zooming in motor car. Another Brit making it big in LA.

shot again, Chris Burden in Santa Ana. One "n," not two.

further coast down, Eleanor Antin's boots. 100 facing the sea. boots to mailboxes everywhere.

      with Allan Sekula's

              Box Car

              During a journey by freight train
              from Santa Barbara to Los Angeles,
              I made a photograph from an open
              box car of a chemical company where
              I had worked two years earlier.
                      –December 1971

1972

Los(t) in the ecology of evil Angel(es)

        remarkable light on five cars, quick dark mission. arrived at Womanhouse in search
of Group Operation
            or, flexible reality. arrived as high art: toasters, quilters, shower caps.

        a reversal of laws

Betye Saer's Aunt Jemima; a further syrup. Red on red; black on black. a syrup of scientific. of size.

            re(claim)ed

How "Easy" was the activity?

                walking along a dry California streambed.
                illustrate but not document.
                      difference in register.

stolen:
        B. Nauman: Perfect Door/Perfect Odor/Perfect Rodo

                        AWAKE
                        again

but I still can teach a plant the alphabet

1973

Mermaid tavern, Topangaside, wildside

      the two of us. back here together, the Los Four, la collective. spirit house.

            what mummy, and all that in *The Long Goodbye*.

            Susan's right: Mobil is a mogul. more than stucco

   little guy de Cointet; fat dick on chalkboard. glass and tie!

        then air condition : wet yr body. wait. when dry: again and again in a new
reality : the permanent arms economy of late capitalism.

the Diebenkorn and Ocean Park: gray blue to field the breaks, surface

1974

quick quick quick quick   hot sand. hot house. a hot dog

           journal, a night with Sophie Rummel, illogical words of Andy's

                      Viva. Viva, but not Las Vegas....

      like desert people, Michael Asher in the empty gallery.
      the white cube on empty. no gas crises here.

      all fire, all flood

a day to flip up yr visor.

1975

A BLVD. CALLED SUNSET

     all (false silence)
     catered to fruit juice, hah. all the way lost to, collect, thoughts, process, as if to say, I can suck you dry. ok.

                                  in sailor's meat, your dick slipped out. everything was gray. I won't break your record. before noon Sunday, out to Ivar's theatre. miraculous, the wind in the bedroom. all in a violet frame, the nighthawk night.

1976

                cars
                    a light terrace
                            fixture

        more shapes on noon
                to have moved between me
                    night paged

        long afternoon of Cassavetes ruin

                        walking upside down
                                with ash
                                        unpaginated

                these directories
                            contain
                            Polaroid method(s)

            so   relax

            as you
                    trust

1977

to see

KILLER OF SHEEP

on the marquee

& again know the future will fall before you've
arrived to
face it

tending forest
           pink pillow, a window telling tales,
                       the great road of gravel, dirt, no
chance,
      how many people hike with you,
                to knots, bays, small shiny stones, throng of
sea birds, wave on palms, referent of not returning,
                     neither gold, crash, an alchemical in balance, a
lone photograph, aching for something mythical, parental, some predestined
gold shower, dwarf dendrites and deer, little woods stand between road and road, chain of
hills, volcanic, nine sisters, oaked, with buttes, rocky,
              up,
                micro falcons, quadrangles, an ocean bound,
thistle, sanicle,
      rewards, post office, bed in church,
                   travel Crespi's footsteps, dry creeks,
salt water, spilled petals chewed, a gnashing sensation, beauty marks and hair clips,
           vertical sensations
           blue crisp
           night cast
           into still
           visor
   a vision, making movements in small time, quick quick, a buckled flight, air
raider, the hawk draft & above,
            elevation, movement in cycles, generations mark, topical ailments,
in bay, spreading gum trees, barks stripped, fallen,
               further, grass fires, oceanic
rockwork, on holiday, drift hair, snazzy sneakers, to take in linear, cormorants, egret
workshop,
      Montaña De Oro then, with father, without,
              amber, a maze, maize, dry
mustard flanking,
     where then, in flowers,
           Pacific,
             myriad of eucalyptus root embankment, from
Islay and Hazard, above bay, at bay.

73

"Night, In the Oaks" borrows phrases from David Bromige's *My Poetry* (Berkeley, CA: The Figures, 1980.) The poem was written in memory of Bromige.

"Via Bixby" refers to the Bixby Bridge on California's Big Sur coast. This poem was written in response to Philip Whalen's "In the Night."

"walk & ferry" is dedicated to Etel Adnan.

"Tea Palinode (18th & Sanchez)" is for Brian Teare.

"Delusion's Enclosure: on Harry Partch (1901 - 1974)" is a long poem based on the life and work of the composer Harry Partch. Born in 1901, Partch established residences for short periods of time in Los Angeles, Oakland, Sausalito, Madison, Urbana, Petaluma, Encinitas, and San Diego, where he died in 1974. He invented the 43-tone scale as well as numerous instruments. I consulted Bob Gilmore's *Harry Partch: A Biography* (New Haven, CT: Yale University Press, 1998); Harry Partch's two books, *Genesis of a Music: An Account of a Creative Work, Its Roots, and Its Fulfillments* (New York: Da Capo, 1974) and *Bitter Music: Collected Journals, Essays, Introductions, and Librettos* (Urbana, IL: The University of Illinois Press, 1991); Jonathan Cott's *Rolling Stones* interview with Partch, reprinted in *Forever Young* (New York: Random House, 1977); and the American Composer's Forum's Innova label's 8-volume *Enclosure* series, edited by Philip Blackburn, dedicated to the writings, music, and films of Harry Partch.

"City Set: Los Angeles Years" is drawn from many sources, but the exhibition catalog *Los Angeles: Birth of an Art Capital* (Paris: Centre Pompidou, 2006) and Richard Cándida Smith's *The Modern Moves West: California Artists and Democratic Culture in the Twentieth Century* (Philadelphia: The University of Pennsylvania Press, 2009) were indispensable resources. The piece was also influenced by a visit to Noah Purifoy's art site in Joshua Tree, California.

"Near Los Osos" is for Caren.

me and Nina, Monica A. Hand
Hagar Before the Occupation | Hagar After the Occupation, Amal al-Jubouri
Pier, Janine Oshiro
Heart First into the Forest, Stacy Gnall
This Strange Land, Shara McCallum
lie down too, Lesle Lewis
Panic, Laura McCullough
Milk Dress, Nicole Cooley
Parable of Hide and Seek, Chad Sweeney
Shahid Reads His Own Palm, Reginald Dwayne Betts
How to Catch a Falling Knife, Daniel Johnson
Phantom Noise, Brian Turner
Father Dirt, Mihaela Moscaliuc
Pageant, Joanna Fuhrman
The Bitter Withy, Donald Revell
Winter Tenor, Kevin Goodan
Slamming Open the Door, Kathleen Sheeder Bonanno
Rough Cradle, Betsy Sholl
Shelter, Carey Salerno
The Next Country, Idra Novey
Begin Anywhere, Frank Giampietro
The Usable Field, Jane Mead
King Baby, Lia Purpura
The Temple Gate Called Beautiful, David Kirby
Door to a Noisy Room, Peter Waldor
Beloved Idea, Ann Killough
The World in Place of Itself, Bill Rasmovicz
Equivocal, Julie Carr
A Thief of Strings, Donald Revell
Take What You Want, Henrietta Goodman
The Glass Age, Cole Swensen
The Case Against Happiness, Jean-Paul Pecqueur
Ruin, Cynthia Cruz
Forth A Raven, Christina Davis
The Pitch, Tom Thompson

Alice James Books has been publishing poetry since 1973 and remains one of the few presses in the country that is run collectively. The cooperative selects manuscripts for publication primarily through regional and national annual competitions. Authors who win a Kinereth Gensler Award become active members of the cooperative board and participate in the editorial decisions of the press. The press, which historically has placed an emphasis on publishing women poets, was named for Alice James, sister of William and Henry, whose fine journal and gift for writing went unrecognized during her lifetime.

TYPESET AND DESIGNED BY MARY AUSTIN SPEAKER

Printed by Thomson-Shore
on 30% postconsumer recycled paper
processed chlorine-free